YOUR KNOWLEDGE HAS

- We will publish your bachelor's and master's thesis, essays and papers

- Your own eBook and book - sold worldwide in all relevant shops

- Earn money with each sale

Upload your text at www.GRIN.com and publish for free

Bibliographic information published by the German National Library:

The German National Library lists this publication in the National Bibliography; detailed bibliographic data are available on the Internet at http://dnb.dnb.de .

Imprint:

Copyright © 2010 GRIN Verlag, Open Publishing GmbH
Print and binding: Books on Demand GmbH, Norderstedt Germany
ISBN: 978-3-668-04415-9

Anna Stumpe

Like Father, Like Son. The Impact of the Hanoverian Family Dispute on British Policy

GRIN Publishing

GRIN - Your knowledge has value

Since its foundation in 1998, GRIN has specialized in publishing academic texts by students, college teachers and other academics as e-book and printed book. The website www.grin.com is an ideal platform for presenting term papers, final papers, scientific essays, dissertations and specialist books.

Visit us on the internet:

http://www.grin.com/

http://www.facebook.com/grincom

http://www.twitter.com/grin_com

Institut für Anglistik und Amerikanistik

Wissenschaftliche Seminararbeit

Zum Proseminar "British Monarchy from Henry VIII to the Present"

Thema:

Like Father, Like Son -

The Impact of the Hanoverian Family Dispute on British Policy

Eingereicht von:

Anna Stumpe

SS 2009

30. September 2010

List of Contents

Appendix

References

1. Introduction

This assignment questions the family dispute within the early Hanoverian court, more precisely those between George Louis, Prince of Brunswick-Luneburg and his son George August, Prince of Wales and how far their relationship influenced governmental and administrative procedures in British domestic and foreign policy. Therefore the timeframe of the early eighteenth century is pertained, that is to say both the reigns of George I (1714- 1727) and George II (1727-1760).

Within the scope of the history of British monarchy, there is a considerable, growing specialist literature on British foreign policy and therefore an increasing interest on the Hanoverian Electorate. Most of the works concentrate on biographical data of George I and George II and historical effects of their political procedures, such as the Glorious Revolution or the Jacobite Rebellions. However, the core theme of this assignment lies in the relationship between both the kings, with relevance to the British monarchy's history and to what extent the Hanoverians have a bearing on imminent British policy.

By contrast, with contemporaries, there is less information on both George I and George II. The amount of information, research and publications continues to fall on the second half of the eighteenth century. In the account of the eighteenth century as a whole, works on the first half do not play a main role but in recent decades an interest in George II looms what calls for the reference to his father, George I, as well.

Especially Jeremy Black's *The Hanoverians: The History of a Dynasty* and *The Oxford Illustrated History of the British Monarchy* by John Cannon and Ralph Griffiths are the most determining research literature to the early Hanoverians. All of these academic works are authoritative accounts to British monarchy guiding through the British history and emphasising George I's and George II's importance to British history, especially George II's importance and independence by focusing on his role in foreign policy.

At first, the research concentrates on the major issues of the family dispute that laid the foundation to the discord in the Hanoverian family. Subsequently, Georges I and II governments are in the centre of attention: the dispute's impact on their actions or the measure of relevance their procedures had on their further disagreement. Here, the focus lies in their domestic and foreign policies, including ministerial and governmental as well as courtly affairs. Eventually, not only the king's disputes but as well the king's impact on British history is resumed.

Lastly here it is important to mention that a complete description of the historical events during the forty-six years that are displayed in this research will not take place. There have only be declared particular events for a wider historical understanding. For more debate on the history of the late seventeenth and eighteenth century the bibliography cited at the end of this research is to be referred to.

2. The Hanoverian Family Dispute

The father-son relationship between the Hanoverians George I and George II has a reputation for being extremely strained, estranged and frigid (Black 2004, Cannon and Griffiths 1992) what can mostly be seen from the fact that their meetings are traversed by choleric quarrels and disputes.

Historians such as Jeremy Black are convinced that the tension between ruler and heir is a classic feature of dynastic politics (cp. Black 2004, 65), but the escalation of their quarrel is not anymore just tensed, but considerably more desperate.

The personal friction between father and son is already established in early years before the reigns of George I or George II and comprised the King's wife and mother of Prince of Wales, Sophia Dorothea of Brunswick-Luneburg. She was the heiress to George William, Duke of Celle. Her relationship to the Swedish count and Hanoverian colonel Philipp Christoph von Königsmarck "did not remain a secret for long" (Black 2004, 57) and as a direct consequence of her adultery, Sophia was detained and confined under her father's care at the manor house of Ahlden, where she was kept until her death. Here, Black mentions that the impact on George II of his parent's divorce is unclear (cp. Black 2004,84), whereas it has to be considered that the early separation from his mother from the year 1692 on, must have essentially influenced the young George. The entire humiliation of his mother led by his grandfather and father, who "was interested in ensuring that George William kept his promise to detain Sophia Dorothea" (Black 2004, 58), must have scarred the prince. Thus, it must be assumed that from early on George I made a major contribution to his son's alienation, discord and impeachment of his parental authority.

George I experienced a secure family background including maternal love and encouragement (cp. Black 2004, 84), but adapted interventions by his father, Ernest August, the Duke of Brunswick-Luneburg. To adduce as a first instance, Ernest August arranged Maria Katharine von Meysenburg, the younger sister of his own mistress, to become his son's mistress after he had made the under-governess of his sister pregnant. Secondly, he introduced primogeniture to enhance the family's position by the undivided inheritance of the eldest son, namely George I. Although Ernest August herewith influenced his son's situation in positive manner securing his succession to the throne, he isolated George from his brothers and made them alienated by the loss of their prospects (cp. Black 2004, 57). The primogeniture then followed George I's marriage to Sophie Dorothea, "a marriage that was a crucial step in the consolidation of the family's interests" (Black 2004, 57).

Considering the procedures that Ernest August had met, it is less surprising for whatever reasons George I made decisions for his son, after all, he himself had never experienced a different paternal education.

Best example and most public clash between father and son is those which revolves around the baptism of George II's son George William. The choice of George Williams' godfather in 1717 is to blame for the struggle. King George I supported the Duke of Newcastle who claimed traditional rights to be the godfather (cp. Cannon and Griffiths 1992, 465), whereas George II has not been in favour of the Lord Chamberlain and wished to have his brother, the Duke of York and Albany, assigned as the godfather at the baptismal ceremonies, instead. The rift between father and son widened because the Duke of Newcastle affirmed that the prince was inclined to fight him. As a consequence, the King arrested and temporarily confined his son from all public ceremonies in which the royal family occasionally appeared, he furthermore was expelled from St. James Palace, the King's royal residence.

With this outcome, the differences between the king and his heir reached the climax. Not only the past had drastically worsened the father-son relationship, also during the reign of George I clashes were continued. Their disputes turned to the major domestic issue, and "fitted into a parliamentary framework" (Black 2004, 62), wherefore the reconciliation of George I and the Prince of Wales most concerned the parliament. The choleric quarrel, as Jeremy Black goes on, "interacted with and seriously worsened the political disputes" (Black 2004, 65). In historian reviews it is widely common that George II did all in his power to encourage opposition to his father's policies. The disputes within the royal family mainly affected British policies at that time, Black says here,

> The ambitions and interests of George I and George II maintained the dynamism of Hanoverian policy; one, however, that was unwise and, in large part, unsuccessful in itself, and a source of concern and anger to numerous British ministers and diplomats (Black 2004, 41).

In what manner the criticism of the both George's governmental and administrative procedures finds expression, how far they differ and how far these differences are concerned with the family disputes, is to be resolved in the following chapter.

3. The Impact on British Politics of the Family Discord

3.1 Court Life

George I's succession to the English throne was not secured from the beginning. Since neither William III and Maria II, nor Queen Anne had any children who could have followed them in the succession to the throne, and Anne being the last heir in the Stuart line, the crown would return to the deposed Roman Catholic James II and his heirs. The Act of Settlement was designed in 1701 to avoid the continuation of the hereditary Stuart heir, therefore it excluded the Catholics and Stuarts out of the British succession to the throne, and instead passed it to the German Protestant cousins, the House of Hanover. Sophia of Hanover, the mother of George I, herewith was placed above them, even if there were relatives whose claims were stronger, and after the death of both Sophia and Queen Anne, George succeeded the English throne in 1714 (cp. Cannon and Griffiths 1992, Black 2004, Sieper 2002).

After George I's difficult succession in terms of the Act of Settlement, he struggled with his new situation and role as the new head of England. Within his early years as King of England, he was faced with numerous problems. First of all and most crucial to his difficulties in his new kingdom was his disinterest and dislike of England, his lack of knowledge of British politics and his obvious preference for Hanover. As the Prussian envoy Friedrich Bonet reported,

> George disliked England, for its language, constitution, political parties and continual importunities for royal favour" (cit. Black 2004, 59).

For that reason, George I did not speak and made little effort to learn the English language (cp. Black 2004, 51). All ministerial documents therefore had to be translated into French and the ceremonial of his coronation had to be explained into Latin (cp. Black 2004, 59). Consequentially, George I felt indisposition in his new home country, wherefore he was unable to develop British national interests (cp. Black 2004, 59) and was more concerned about Hanoverian affairs. This in turn means that, on the one hand, he excluded himself from British society. As Beattie describes, George I was a man with an extreme shyness of crowds, a dislike of formality and a preference to a quite and retired life. He always remained in background, never courted popular acclaim and rarely showed himself to his people (cp. Beattie 1966, 26-27). Therefore, George I was faced with his extreme unpopularity among the British society:

> The British found their new ruler to an unglamorous elderly gentleman (Cannon and Griffiths 1992, 466).

He always remained a passive actor in court life what "allowed him the more easily to indulge his preference for privacy and informality" (Beattie 1966, 27).

In contrast to his father, the prince, who had accompanied his father in 1714, was closely linked to all of these matters. He was very much in evidence in court life (cp. Beattie 1966, 27) and with great knowledge of the English language. Therefore, the king's son and his daughter-in-law, Caroline of Ansbach-Bayreuth, were in great advantage and of much popularity within the English society nearly leading court life (cp. Beattie 1966, 28).

This imbalance and difference of the character traits of father and son are without any doubt the reason for the never ending struggle between them. As well king George I's jealousy of his son's popularity and the fear his son could completely lead social court life, further worsened the conflict. The king obviously disliked and distrusted his son such that he would never led him control over the crown's patronage, despite the fact that George always has been willed to remain a passive actor of court life. Beattie offers an explanation for the father's dislike, he says, "the prince's open declaration of political independence drove a much more serious breach between them" (Beattie 1996, 28). That was, in his anger, to seriously emphasise the difference from his father. On this occasion, in 1716 Sir Robert

Walpole[1] wrote to Earl James Stanhope (cit. in Beattie 1966, 28),

> He maintained a court in a style previously unknown in the reign and welcomed to it men of every political persuasion. Men out of sympathy or out of favour with the administration, tories and disgruntled whigs, flocked to [...] be welcomed graciously by the prince and the princess.

This official rebellion against his father made the prince the head of the opposition against him, the king.

3.2 Domestic Policies

The parliamentary monarchy was a product of the Glorious Revolution, and successfully responded to changes in the political world and the interests and abilities of individual monarchs. The participation of parliament in policy formation developed and formed a new stage in the longstanding relationship between crown and parliament. Especially Sir Robert Walpole managed to demonstrate to the crown that a parliamentary monarchy is helpful to provide stability, continuity, peace and lower taxes (cp. Black 2004, 46).

But actually, George I did not want a coalition government, above all because of his hatred of the Tories, but he cooperated with the government. This is said to his lack in decisiveness, charisma and wiliness (cp. Black 2004, 62). In comparison with his contemporaries, Louis XIV of France or Peter the Great of Russia, George I had no attempts to win such reputation, but he was always determined and ambitious to maintain his rule and to keep with his position.

George II instead was only determined to be his own master and "was making a serious attempt to intervene in the process of government" (cp. Black 2004, 90). From his accession in 1727, he had his own sources of information and opinions, and was known for royal preferences within his reign. To not let anybody dictate him, he wished to control all governmental activities, intervened in the process of government, undermined ministerial positions in parliament and only employed favourites (cp. Black 2004, 49; 98). Cannon and Griffiths says here that he had no likings for George I's ministers" (cp. 1992, 469). They are no certain evidences to these facts, but strong beliefs that George II made in his serious attempts ventures to reduce the need for governmental borrowing and the dependence on parliamentary

---

[1] Sir Robert Walpole was a leading Whig statesman who is considered to the office of the first British Prime Minister. He served through both the reigns of George I and George II. His tenure is dated from 1721 when he obtained the post of the First Lord of Treasury, and governed through 1742. His

grants within his reign.

But one thing that father and son shared as a similarity was the reliance in the Whig ministry, nevertheless. They both relied on the Whigs and harboured resentment against the Tories whose opinions conflicted with their royal interests,

> George I and George II suspected the Tories of Jacobite inclinations and were alienated by Tory opposition to their commitments to continental power politics, and by Tory hostility to continental Protestantism (Black 2004, 44).

They, nevertheless, sought Tory help though only in order to serve Whig ministries and measures. But they were no more absolute reliance on the Whig ministry as they were intra-party disputes as a struggle for power within the party. Trigger for this dispute was the king's foreign policy. While Walpole and his brother-in-law Townshend represented the opinion that George I was much more concerned about Hanoverian foreign policies than interested in British political affairs, Stanhope and Sunderland took party for the king. With the intrigue of Lord Sunderland against Lord Townshend, the confrontation reached its peak. Sunderland removed Townshend from his position as the Secretary of State for the Northern department and placed him in less influential office. As Townshend then also these Lieutenancy of Ireland was ousted, Walpole resigned with him and joined the opposition (Beattie 1966, Black 2004, Cannon and Griffiths 1992). This had a drastic effect on King George I, because the Whig opposition clustered around the prince, wherefore "George I was forced to emerge from his habitual and preferred seclusion and replace his son as the leader of the social world" (Beattie 1966, 30). To encounter his limitation of power, he lent full support to the rival ministerial group, which eventually led to Townshend's dismissal and Walpole's resignation. The prince received Walpole with open arms despite the fact that he was always said to hate his father's ministry.

Simultaneously the split in the Whig party, the split in the royal family expanded as well.

Not only that familiar hostilities have significantly influenced policy so far, the split greatly weakened the administration in 1717. Father and son entered in competition with each other, what forced the members of the government to "a declaration of allegiance to one side or another - to the king and government or to the prince and the opposition" (Beattie 1966, 34). But whereas the reconciliation between the king and his heir had never been more than formal (cp. Cannon and Griffiths 1992, 469),

---

administration is regarded as the longest in British history, also as the most eventful (see ch. 3.2).

the split among the leading Whig politicians was resolved in 1720 with the return of Walpole and Townshend in office.

Comprising, it can already be said that the family situation within the Hanoverian royal family had considerable influence on political affairs, more precisely on the government, the ministers and ministerial decisions. Still under the banner of George I, the ministers seemed to be more anxious about the improvement of the father-son relationship than in the attending to their actual duties. Additionally, they entangled themselves in dispute and caused a deep division among the ministry. Especially Robert Walpole was endeavoured to merge father and son in a more detached relationship to secure himself in office.

In this context it is important to mention that the relationship between the Prince of Wales and his wife, Caroline of Ansbach-Bayreuth, had an impact on political affairs in equal measure. Only with the Queen's encouragement and his "powerful ally in the new Queen" (Morris 1874,79) Walpole could return in office and cement his position for the first fifteen years of George II's reign. Caroline of Ansbach-Bayreuth was considered as a woman of grace, beauty, cleverness and rationality (cp. Morris ,79), who was able to govern the king by the skilful choice of opportunities and arguments:

> She instilled notions into the King's mind in such a subtle way that the thought they were his own, and thus she was wont to govern the King without his knowing that he was being governed (Morris 1874, 80).

Likewise his son who was strongly influenced by his wife, George I was under the influence of one of his mistresses. At this point it becomes clear that father and son were equal in their intension to women, and not as different as they thought of themselves they were. Despite being on good terms with his wife and allowing the impact on him, the Prince of Wales was not prevented from having mistresses either, but he was careful not to allow his women to compromise his political position. After the death of Queen Caroline in 1737, this intension changed. George II settled down into a domestic relationship with his mistress Amalia Sophie Marianne von Walmoden. He made this woman, who had easy access to him, Countess of Yarmouth with whom she became an influential political force conveying ideas to George. This, the role of the Countess of Yarmouth, is comparable to George I's mistress, Marianne von der Schulenburg. She was benefited by South Sea Company to strengthen the king's support to the company, wherefore she was not regarded as a influential political force, but as an immediate access to the king's decisions (cp. Black 2004, 107).

3.3 Foreign Policies

Regarding the British foreign policy during the early Hanoverian reigns from 1714 to 1760, the effort to gain political stability was the most important concern. Being pragmatists, they knew stability was something that had to be fought for (cp. Black 2004, 53). Presumably, they both were focused with a time of rebellion and wars and they, eventually, only survived, as Black says, because they displayed level-headedness and less panic what is another but small evidence to some shared characteristics that made them more related to each other than they ever proclaimed. For once, both George I and George II agreed with each other:

> Both [...] were interested in the details of foreign policy and sought to use British resources to help secure gains for Hanover (Black 2004, 40).

In looking at Britain's external position in the eighteenth century, imperial identity and expansion were the dominant factors, mainly concentrated on the Atlantic. Within this focus and as the citations mentions, Hanoverian security and interests were of great concern to Georges I and II. This, as earlier explained, was the cause of the Whig Split, and in general the source of concern and anger to numerous British ministers and diplomats. Thomas, Duke of Newcastle, the most influential minister to British foreign policy from 1744 to 1756, was devoted to invent an international system that would deter attack on Hanover. This, Newcastle's concern, indicated the shifting nature of British concern with Hanover. Sir Robert Walpole was far less concerned with Hanoverian security and interests than Newcastle was, but he was, nevertheless, aware of the implications of the Hanoverian connections for British foreign policy (cp. Black 2005, pp. 304-306). As Black (2004, 41) explains, "the consistent and readily apparent Hanoverian ambitions of both kings made their British ministries vulnerable to domestic criticism and Hanover to foreign attack".

Within his first five years of accession, George I was not only faced with the division of the Whigs and the disallowance of the Tories, he was moreover at war with Spain provoked by the Triple Alliance he had founded in agreement with France and the United Provinces in 1716. Besides, Hanoverian policy always struggled with the Baltic powers, Denmark, Sweden, Prussia and Russia. Than, as the king of Great Britain, George I saw opportunities for expansion because of the weaknesses of Swedish empire on the one hand, but on the other he feared the rising power of Russian and Prussian empires (cp. Black 2005, 304). That is how it came to the clash over Baltic policy what can be considered as the first breach within the British political stability.

But the worst problem he and his kingdom's political stability was faced with were the three major Jacobite rebellion in 1715,1719 and 1745 that turned both the governments into military and political crisis. The Stuarts, James and his son Charles Stuart called the Old and the Young Pretender, tried to regain the British throne, and France as a catholic nation supported the Stuart's claim to the throne. Charles Stuart, the Bonnie Prince Charlie, wanted to overthrow Hanoverian rule in Britain and made the attempt to claim the throne for his father who has not been keen in becoming involved in military campaigns anymore. James and Charles instigated rebellion in Scotland, where support for Jacobitism was stronger than in England. But both "the Fifteen" and the second rebellion in 1719, "the Nineteenth", crushed. The Jacobites were poorly equipped and therefore easily defeated by the British artillery. With France supporting the Stuarts' claim to the throne, the Anglo-French alliance was dissolved and Anglo-French negotiation became urgent for both, Britain and Hanover (cp. Black 2005, Cannon and Griffiths 1992). Just outpaced these turbulences, George I was soon faced with the next crisis: the South Sea Bubble in 1720. The South Sea Company was a joint stock company founded in 1711 hat was promised a monopoly of all trade to the Spanisch colonies in South America in exchange for taking over and consolidating the national debt raised by the War of Spanish Succession (1701-1714). This caused the war against Spain and financial ruin. The royal family was deeply involved, personally and publicly. The procession with the financial crisis made the king and his ministers still more unpopular and the tension within the family even more fractious.

Within the South Sea Bubble again Walpole was left at the most important figure in the administration, and arranged the decline of political power of the monarchy what made the modern system of cabinet government led by (prime) ministers and George I less and less involved in government. Again because of his lack in decisiveness and perseverance, and because of his lack of British political agenda (cp. Black 2004, Cannon and Griffith 1992).

In another way as well, admittedly George II has not been as keenly interested in Hanover as his father was, but the interest in Hanoverian security, interests and expansionism slightly recurred under George II who operated trough Hanoverian government (and through the British envoy in St. Petersburg) to contradict the anti-French emphasis of the British monarchy. For the reason that he was still not willed to support the Tories and unable to dominate the ministry as he had wished to. In this course, Jacobite activities increased again what caused the outbreak of war with France in 1743. The situation worsened in 1745 with the third major Jacobite Rising. In the Battle of Culloden at Culloden Moor in 1746 the Duke of Cumberland raised an army that was able to defeat the outnumbered Jacobites. The aftermath of the Jacobite rebellion was the destruction oft the Jacobite hopes. Their risings ended after more than fifty years if continuous disappointment and adversity wherefore the claim to the throne was no longer in dispute and the Jacobites, and their Tory supporters, not anymore regarded as within the body of politic (cp. Cannon and Griffiths 1992, Morris 1988, BBC History). Most important, the aftermath managed that "the Hanoverian dynasty was finally and explicitly accepted by most of the political nations as representing the aspirations and security of the realm" (Black 2004, 100).

As little as George II showed interests in his royal role in the Royal Society, he was keenly interested in military affairs. He was determined to control Britain's military patronage, but "also kept a close eye on military developments in other countries followed European campaigns with great interest" (Black 2004, 103). Black justifies this attitude with the king's character:

> George associated the army with his *gloire*, and believed that the military reviews he conducted were the most obvious and impressive display of his power and importance (Black 2004, 103).

George II's military interest was not comparable with those of his family members. Admittedly, his father, George I, was once working hard in the metier of rulership and followed his father's interests what included courage in military operations, but during his reign, he was less affected by the army. Solely Frederick Louis, Prince of Wales, George II's oldest son and the father of the latter George III, mirrored his interests. Not only he also mirrored the relationship of Georges I and II. The bond between Frederick and George II was nearly as difficult as it was years ago with his father and grandfather. Frederick soon developed political links with opposition Whigs crucially effecting the fall of Sir Robert Walpole in 1742 and provoking the consolidation of the dispute between father and son. The notorious dislike worsened with George II's obvious preference for Cumberland, whom he made an authoritarian militarist during the Jacobite rebellions.

The personal interest of George II in the army is regarded as a major nuisance to his British ministers (cp. Black 2004, 103). Even in his last years he was still determined to resist ministerial appointments, but faced with the size of government business, he slowly prepared to only supervise all that he wished to control and he eventually left politics and government to his ministers. He, instead, was still more concerned about foreign policy, and the fact that he had no political agenda was important to the development of political stability. Despite this reputation, he was the last British king to fight in a battle on British soil.

4. Conclusion

As the research should have made clear, the family of the House of Hanover is traversed by family disputes, quarrels and differences across generations. Although royal scandals - as it could be called like this - are in British history not uncommon, and reoccurred among the Hanoverians' successors. But those of the Hanoverian House had in contrary to others in British royal history not only an immense impact on the family situation, but rather on social, economic and especially on political events and procedures.

Thus, especially the scandal of the House of Windsor's Prince Charles and his former wife Lady Diana is well known. Lady Diana, one of Britain's most fondly remembered and beloved members of the royal family, admitted in an BBC interview in 1995 her love affair with Major James Hewitt, a polo player and close friend. Three years ago, a phone conversation between Prince Charles and his mistress Camilla Parker Bowles is tapped. Within this conversation, Prince Charles reveals his affair by sexual explicit allusions. Camilla Parker-Bowles then succeeded to be the woman alongside Charles after Lady Di's tragic death in 1997.

But these events differ substantially from those occurring at the time of Georges I and II. While the scandal of unfaithfulness in the Nineties played a major role, the real scandal in the eighteenth century was the behaviour of the governance and the incidental immense impact on the stability of the government which at that time - after the Glorious Revolution - was still in its early stages of development. To cap it all, neither George I nor George II showed keenness in English affairs, wherefore they were instrumental in contributing not only to disputes in the ministry, but also to those between country like those between the UK and France what lasts until recent days. Thereby, neither the quarrels between Georges I and II nor those between George II and Frederick Louis were reconciled, this has only been officially in order to keep up appearances.

The Hanoverianism not only offered problematic situations. George I lead divisive politics, but initially and eventually seemed to have helped to make the political system work effectively, side by side with what Walpole initiated as the cabinet government. On cultural and intellectual terms, several scientific literature is spoken of George I as an important figure of the early Enlightenment. He planned the university at Göttingen, founded the Regius Professorships of modern history at the universities of Oxford and Cambridge and granted the latter with the purchase of the internationally famous library of John Moore whose collection of nearly 29.000 books and 1790 manuscripts doubled the stock of the university library (cp. Black 2004, 79). His personality, therefore, is not only proof to the disputes with his son and ministers. George II, as well, can not only be regared as obstinate and martial tempered. He marked a major turning point in the history of the dynasty and ended a "cosmopolitan period" as Black says (cp. 2004, 111). In the matter of cultural preferences in the age of Baroque monarchy, he echoes Italianate and French culture and style. All in all, despite the turbulences during the Jacobite Risings, the South Sea Bubble, the Seven Years War or the Great Northern War, the reverse side of their reigns has to be regarded in equal measure and offers good publicity, as well.

References

- Baker-Smith, Veronica. Royal Discord: The Family of George II. London: Athena Pres, 2008.

- Beattie, J.M. "The Court of George I and English Politics, 1717-1720". The English Historical Review, Vol. 81, No. 318. Oxford: Oxford Univ. Press, 1966. pp. 26-37.

- *BBC History.* „The Making of the Union. The Jacobites and the Union". Web. 19.06.2010. http://www.bbc.co.uk/history/scottishhistory/union/features_union_jacobites.shtml

- Black, Jeremy. "The Hanoverians. The History of a Dynasty". Dynasties. London: Hambledon and London, 2004.

- Black, Jeremy. "Hanover and British Foreign Policy". The English Historical Review, Vol. 120, No. 468. Oxford: Oxford Univ. Press, 2005.

- Green, Vivian, Hubert Howard. The Hanoverians 1714-1815. London: Arnold, 1976

- Morris, Edward Ellis. The Early Hanoverians. London: Longmans Green & Co., 1886 (2008 Reprint).
- Robertson, Grant C., Charles William Chadwick Oman. England under the Hanoverians. London: Methuen, 1944.

- *The Longman Companion to Britain in the Eighteenth Century, 1688-1820.* Ed. Jeremy Gregory. London: Longman, 2000.

- *The Oxford Illustrated History of the British Monarchy.* Eds. John Cannon, Ralph Griffiths. Oxford: Oxford Univ. Press, 1992.

YOUR KNOWLEDGE HAS VALUE